SCARS THAT SPEAK

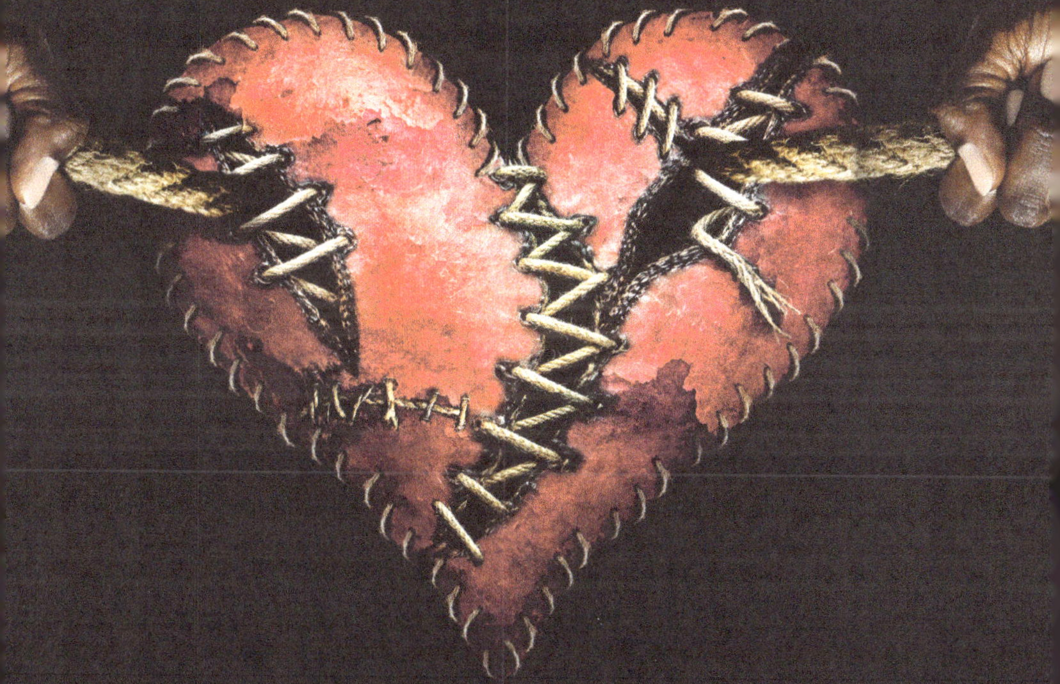

A Poem Collection of Brokenness, Survival, and the Truth Beneath the Silence

SHAYLA JONES

For the scars we carry—
and the courage it takes to let them speak.

Contents

"Healing takes time, and asking for help is a courageous step."
-Mariska Hargitay

"The wound is the place where the light enters you."
-Rumi

*"Although the world is full of suffering,
it is also full of the overcoming of it."*
-Helen Keller

Foreword

We first met Shayla nine years ago at a local domestic violence shelter where we all worked part-time. Even then, she stood out—warm, engaging, and a natural leader. From the very beginning, it was clear that Shayla wasn't simply there to work a shift; she was there to make an impact. Over time, our professional connection grew into something deeper. Today, Shayla is not just a former colleague. She is family.

What has always defined Shayla is her strength. Throughout her life, she has faced hardships that would have stopped most people in their tracks, yet she continually finds a way to rebuild and move forward. We've watched her navigate challenges with remarkable courage, turning moments of pain into opportunities for growth. Shayla doesn't just endure—she evolves.

This book reflects that evolution. Her story will speak to many—especially women who feel lost in their struggles and unsure of what tomorrow might hold. Shayla's journey shows that even in the most difficult seasons, renewal is possible. When life breaks apart, she finds a way to create something new, something stronger, something more hopeful.

But her resilience is only part of what makes her extraordinary. Shayla has always been a steady presence for others. She shows up with compassion, encouragement, and unwavering support—whether for a colleague, a friend, or someone she's meeting for the first time. She has a unique ability to comfort others even when she is carrying her own battles, a testament to her character and her generous heart.

Shayla's openness in this book is a gift. Her words will uplift, empower, and remind readers that healing is within reach. She offers her story not for sympathy, but as a beacon—guiding others who may be searching for hope in their own difficult moments.

We are endlessly proud of Shayla—not just for writing this book, but for living a life marked by courage, compassion, and transformation. Her journey will touch countless lives, just as she has touched ours.

Shayla, we love you beyond words.

With admiration and gratitude,
Camille Young & Doris Gillette

This collection contains themes of emotional pain, trauma, self-harm, and mental health struggles. These poems are reflections of lived experiences and are shared with honesty and care. Reader discretion is advised.

If you or someone you know is struggling, please consider seeking support from a trusted individual or professional.

Call or text 988 to reach the 24/7 Suicide and Crisis Lifeline.

Scars Within

Heavy thoughts.
A mind at war with itself.

Mistake

It was a mistake

I didn't mean to cut that deep
Just needed to scratch the surface

I didn't mean to pull the trigger
Just needed to feel/hold the gun

I didn't meant to take that many pills
Just needed a temporary escape

I didn't mean to jump from that high
Just needed to be at the top for once

I didn't mean to hang for that long
Just needed to know what it feels like to hold my head up

I didn't mean to crash my car
Just needed to know how it feels to let go

I didn't mean to drown
Just needed to see how long I could hold my breath

Then a mistake,

Now reality.

Drowning in Emotion

I can't catch my breath
Eyes flood with distorted vision/sight
Ears muffled with rants of self-disgust

I can't breathe
Pain progressed to panic
Breathing taken for granted
Even when not wanted

Slow breaths, in and out, tense and distressed
Burning of rage, fury and gloom
Struggle to regulate as stable
Rise of tension and stress

Lungs full of pain and tears
In and out of consciousness
Awareness begins to slip away
Peace overtakes me

Drowned in my pain

Beatless Heart or Cardiac Arrest

You're heavy
You're burdened
You're sicken
You're overwhelmed

You're sad and disappointed
You're angry and helpless
You're scarred and bruised
You're hardened and guarded

You bleed out when it can't be kept in
You beat fast when shaken in fear and no wins
You throb when the pain is very intense
You beat slow when breath is in suspense

Anxiety takes over if not cautious when handling
Worries can cause overload, restlessness and fatigue
Disgust for self keeps you cold, noncommittal and withdrawn
Jealousy fuels emotional self-sabotage and poor self-esteem

You will be broken in many places, never to be the same
Nicked and dented from fights, day after day
Discolored and blemished with lifelessness, exhaustion and shame
Constricted and warped from irreparable damage, suffering that's on replay

Heart, the thermometer of life, soon to be still
Longing to be loved to life and experience all the frills
In due time, life will be lost and out of reach
Looks of the heart, evident that life has me beat

Why?

Am I worthy to be chosen?
 Why would you not want me
Perfection, I tried to maintain
Now stained
Will you overlook the shame
I am still the same

Privilege and honor, your affiliation
Not for all, just an approved selection
Branded and bonded with distinction
Committed for life
Serving for social change
Father, mothers, sisters - highest scholars

Kind-hearted and giving
Last thought is one's self
Ally is all that is desired
Network in familiar colors
My heart is large for sisterhood
But known to very few

Raised to mirror sharpness
Dull, my life has become
Prestige is discernible
Ineligible is your stature
Inspiration follows her trail
Confidence, you lack all

Undeserving of the connection
Shameful outcast of the family
Unsuitable to carry on the legend
Weak and weighted with uncertainty
Shamble or success is the toss up
Time yields the fortune

Internal Rage

Mad, are we?
Bitter and broken
Irritable and insensitive
Ready to spit vile on anyone within reach

No one understands
The yells and screams
I have to swallow
The tears, tightness in chest
Sped up heart beat, deep breaths taken

I'm angry, pissed, disappointed
How dumb can you be
Thoughts came to pass
No secret now

The fire inside, wants to attack, fight and kick
Take down every threat, enemy and foe
Guard is up, I am my only protection
Die trying, or surrender silently

Cold, sharp and short
Heartless, blackened and scarred
Beats for survival, lifeless passion for less
Hands up, give in, best of your reality

I have been mistaken for someone of no importance
As if, easily thrown off course
Swaying, no longer anchored
Lost, wandering, forgotten and diminishing

Release before you get sick
Let it out, or again be tricked
No more fake smiles
Internal light dims more, day after day

21

Farewell, My Love

You were never really mine
Stealing someone else's time

My heart was invested
My emotions time-tested

Rollercoaster of feelings and urges
Overwhelmingness constantly emerges

Cold, broken, bitter, withdrawn
Now crying until the day is gone

No relief subsides this pain
Only temporarily scarred veins

You were my true remedy
Needing and wanting you endlessly

Ecstasy left lingering
Unfortunately now dwindling

Time spent, none left to share
Realizing never will I compare

Silence is an ultimate killer
Left on edge in this thriller

Once lover of your soul, heart in hand
Now purposeless, washed away sand

Little Me

You will wonder, why you?
Haven't you been through enough
You wish you were told things will get better
Your heart was broken so young
You will endure even more pain along the way
Will you ever get the man or money?
Kids and the white picket fence?
Many degrees but still not content
Jobs where you are making a difference
Still not enough and accomplished from within despite plenty of references
Hold on, they say
You are the one in your own way

Will you ever catch a break, you wonder
Will your knight and shining armor come to your rescue
Will someone hold your heart with care
Will someone stimulate your mind, gently and with concern
Will you heal just to be hurt again

Or will you be empowered by the pain
Determined to not be defeated
Radical enough to break out of your cage
Committed to the cause
Figure out why all this work and still no gain
Hold on, they say
You are the one in your own way

You will second guess every decision
You did not have a great options to witness
You will quiver at change
Why can't things just be the same
But better.

Flow

Get out of my heart.
Rather feel you near this vein.
The pain. The anxiety.
Hate feeling like I'm going insane.

I'm tired of crying.
Nothing seems sharp enough to kill off the sense of dying.
Inside. Outside. Nothing seems to subside...

The rage, anger, hopelessness
My caged mind and it's brokenness

Red is what I see. Drip and get out of me.
Relief is what you bring.
Sometimes it stings.

Running out of space.
Scars on top of scars.
But the feeling doesn't stop.
Cut and cut because happiness seems too far.

I'm tired of fighting.
The blowback is more than I can handle.
Just every now and again.
I must vandal.

My body. A temple but weak.
Illustrates that I'm a freak.
Misunderstood by my own kind.
Put a label on it, and watch the decline.

Depressed. Sleeping all day.
Cutting, just simply moves the gloom away.

In Memory of W.C.W.

When your heart hurts, an indescribable pain
When someone asks, and you can't simply explain
Confusion sets in, and my charm seems in vain

When out in public, laughs come easy yet somewhat forced
When what once brought joy, peace, relief and a sense of free
Is now not enough, but tough

Like my breath,
I can't breathe
In the sea of emotions,
The take over from the ocean.

I try to grip
I try to get a handle
My hands slip
And no one is around to see me hit, the pit

But it's ok, I say.
Things must be this way.

I'm free.
Let me be.

Just take ...
A shot for love.
A shot for peace.
A shot for joy.
And a shot, for family and me.

Perfect Pain

Gripped by the throat
Slowly my breath eloped
Pain in my chest
My heart is arrest
Eyes filled with rage, pity, agony
This can't be my reality
Feeling of betrayal, disloyal is the game
Family, friends and foe are to blame
Not sure how to recover
My norm has become to suffer
Guarded and gated, for no recurrence
Pick on someone your own size,
I need a divergence
The perfect smile, perfect style
All elements to check off my file
All the swag, wanting to be tagged
With his last name and bragg
What once seemed perfect
Cuts deep, salt in the wound, now is suspect
Broke my heart, shattered my faith, bruised my ego
Ache, throb, pain, I beg, please go

Self-hate

Too thin
Too dark
Too short

Not a wild factor
Not eye candy
Not an exquisite piece

Hard to let go Hard
to leave it be
Hard to let things flow

Doesn't stand out in the crowd
Doesn't complement well
Doesn't surrender without rebuttal

Always tainted and scarred
Always compliments twisted to criticism
Always judged for every grudge

Cry baby can't speak up for self
Cry baby can't express with words
Cry baby can't diffuse turbulence in heart and mind

(Mind on a rant)
Self-sabotage, self-inflict, self-hopelessness
Guarded soul, guilty conscious, groundless foundation
Insecure heart, insignificant memories, indifferent decisions

Fragile being, fickle mindset, faceless presence Bitter
gloom, broken spirit, beaten
Pity party thrower, pretty-less body, panicky under pressure

(Just know)
You will never will be enough
Things will never change
So never expect anything better

You will never be chosen
You are not considered a prize
You're a settlement for a temporary case

Self-Sabotage

I am not enough, not worthy, unfit
Downplaying achievements, it never quits

Pushing away the attractable good
Wimply walking away, from where I once stood

Fear of being hurt, rejected, abandoned
Through the closest exit, you left standin'

Before your chance to get away and leave
Push away, get away, then only left to grieve

Undeserving of any success, imposter described
My new norm, here to stay, the usual vibe

Overwork but still procrastinate, thanks anxiety
Pressure, more pressure coming at me from society

Competent, are you really, do you care
Avoidance seems the best choice and fair

Fear of failing, being a big disappointment
Missed my calling, awaiting reappointment

Socialized to be weak, quiet, only seen
Truly, it is you, do not deny, find that inner

Probation

Another number in the system
Constantly supervised, under surveillance
Stripped of rights and freedom
Taken for granted, now you are the assailant

Main topic of discussion
Many stares, lots of judgement
Mandated conditions to stay in line
Never would have thought, life as is to this extent

Cost of an accident
Depth increases, low to high
Punishment fit the crime
Legal system seems justified

Counseling assigned, assessed, reported
Still remained in the community
Rehabilitating, with a leash
Could have been worse, not given this opportunity

Held accountable for bad habits
Complying under a microscope
Choices lead to consequences, good or bad
Walking the fine line of life is a slippery slope

Guardian vs Guardrail

You waited patiently to attack at the right time
Subtle, almost sneaky; clothed in an experience of prime

Ready to pounce, with intent to destroy and devour
Dark and left alone, incapacitated of strength and power

No mercy for this body, surroundings and materials
Eager to show reign, with a tough exterior

Unknown of the soul inside, protected, with pride
Special, one of a kind, for many she is eyed

Vulnerable, meek, giving and mellow
Precious to many, his angel drifted within the meadow

Alcohol/Guardrail

You plotted and schemed
Plan was in the works for quite some time
Festering, planted, unable to be plucked

Disguised in all my favorites
Overtaken when alone, no guard around
So you thought

Protected in His love
Willing to allow, you devil, to get close
Only tapped, and shaken, not taken

Take all possessions and materials
Isolated and sat down, separated due to shame
Work was valued, now work to stay afloat

He has the ultimate say
I am one of his own
You can't have me

Evident of His purpose, my purpose
His plans are what's best for me
Armored for every battle

Scars That Stayed Too Long

*Some things lingered
long after they should have left.*

Too Sensitive

How can you rate sensitivity
Maybe it is you that is insensitive
Is it my fault that you are heartless
Is it my fault that I care

I have feelings
Should I not express
Is it me that is too harsh
Should I not address

Ruthless are your words
Cut deep, never superficial
Actions, cold and distant
Callous demeanor, as very official

Indifferent to pleasure and pain
I felt all points of adversity
Contained and reserved to the core
I, often overflowing with emotion imperfectly

Dismissive of words and gestures
Pressured to be hard and fair
Rumbling frustration turned to disgust
Understanding of myself I attempt to bare

Settled and stubborn at heart
I am flexible, adjusting to being unheard
Not simple-minded just complicated
Closed shut-off, lines never blurred

Flowers to Weeds

Beauty starts to diminish
As your fixation starts to waver

Scent begins to become stale
As your taste for me becomes disgust

Petals withered and wimped
As your attentiveness becomes inconsistent

Life becomes less lively
As you give care to what is superior

Roots rot and become dry
As you rehydrate for the main attraction

Intimate synthesis at a sudden stop
As temperatures polarize to the extremes

Posture once kept, now slumped
As strength lessens with more inactivity

Pollination at a halt, diseased and cold
As pests bother, color fades, petals shrivel

Once a strikingly beautiful flower
Now a withered, lifeless hideous weed

Fumbled/Turned Over

You wanted me
You chased me
You caught me

Picked out of many
Possessed me with passion
But only for a period

Distraction in disguise
Eyes begin to wander
Mind loses focus on me

Sudden loss of control
Buckling under pressure
No longer in your grasp

Swarmed by opposition
Mishandled me with lack of care
Up for grabs, passed to next

Stolen is the claim
Intercepted with no guard
Trapped with no escape

Defensive you become
Charged with guilt because of me
Out of bounds seems safer

Goaltending for me not a thought
It is not worth the lost
Free throw what was once precious

Fouling for me was taking a chance
Penalty not so great
Loose ball, now your mistake

You once screened for me
Protected me as a good score
Carried me with no violations

But now, ball momentarily dead
Timeout arrests the play
Shot clock releases the inevitable

Now anyone else's game.

The Firsts to Leave/ 3 Exits

Head of the household
You left me for another
Every other, this day and that day
You made another someone a mother

Replaced and left behind
Money given, filled a mangled heart
In search for complementary suitor
More shattering, dart after dart

Dream come true, lover of my soul
My peace of mind from deep within
Ecstatic chemistry when touched
Stares easily undressed us to bare skin

Comforted when cried
Still never worth much of your time
Secret, camouflaged in disguise
Delusional to think it would last a lifetime

Only and around for a weeks
Questioning mothering abilities
Homewrecker, adulterer, not fit for parent
Along would come overwhelming hostilities

Yet you left so abruptly, painfully, quick
Even though I questioned whether I'd want you to stay
If I was equipped, in my prime or ready
Controversial doubt, the burden that I weigh

No choice of mine.
You left me first.

Father.
Fond lover.
Few months nesting mini me.

Puzzle

This piece does not fit
With all that's happening
Burden dressed in the same colors
Attracting the right feelings of relief
This is why this piece should sit

This piece does not fit
It keeps coming back to mine
Seems like the best conclusion
Unique solution like none other
Eyes, mind, heart intertwined like a twisted trick

This piece does not fit
Many other options to try
Turn your focus, other directions to steer
So definite, others would not understand
Smooth transition, get ready for that click (empty that clip)

This piece does not fit
Destiny and accomplishments still within reach
Do not give up, time has been favorable
Have hope and faith plus twice as much work
Getting to the end takes battling self inside and out

This piece does not fit
Not knowing how to live
Coward solution of quick death
Easy escape to avoid the potential
Fear of the unknown

This piece has to fit
Selfish, self-less act, burden ridden
Others move on carelessly
Grand finale, last piece of the story
Most suitable ending to a colorful, traumatic puzzle

20 Years Later

A number of degrees
But every man seems to flee
Still that insecure scared smile
Obvious you are the problem, still, child

Broken, cracked, shattered in many places
Starting over is best, you must face this
Severed ties, fractured relationships
My life, I need help, steady losing my grip

Accomplished or just good on paper
If they only knew, once they pulled back the layers
No kids, no man, solely ol' teacher
Open up, let your guard down, let someone know you deeper

Embarrassed, am I not enough
Make up, hair and clothes, someone soon will call my bluff
Miserable, anxious, lonely and bitter
More often than not, I was a life quitter

Hoping to gather myself and see the light
Every day, every hour, every minute is a fight
Reflect and reset, the next 20 years is now
Shakingly, anxiously, I am ready to be crowned

Present but Absent

Nurturing but naive
Supportive but stuck
Friendly but fragile
Present but poisoned
Wholeheartedly involved but weak
Bruised and scarred
Coped with what was not yours
A selfless giver to others
Stingy with caring for oneself
Scandalous behaviors displayed
Heavy shadows lurked behind
Far from a disciplinarian, when due
Walked over time and time again
Age is no truth-teller of growth
Emotion stunted from way back when
Little girl caught in the cycle
See saw, roller coaster of life
Chewed up, swallowed, no bounce back

Roll model, of what to do different

I needed more
Money and gifts, all for show
Hurt and haunted
Lost and in constant limbo
Emotionally juvenile
Perception distorted
Sensitive to touch and view
Many looks of insecurity
Customs not changed
Cycle of self-defeat not broken
Unwise choices, time after time

Awkward hugs and kisses
Uncomfortable storytelling
Connection fickle and wavering
Trust two-timing, full of doubt
Strife, confliction inevitably to avoid
Pity my soul, determine to be the difference

Money Money Money

Made are divisions in class, status and opportunity
Made in slow time, and spent in no time
Made to be clean and crisp, yet has potential to be grimy and dirty
Made to beg, plead, what is put in my hand
Money molds thoughts, speaks volumes and shapes behavior

Others lose their mind over you
Often kill, steal and destroy for you
Overly fearful to be without you
Only my pockets, truly, can express their emptiness
Offering only temporary comfort, for I am indebted to many

Not enough jobs have made me content with you
Noticeably, I handle you with care
Nifty, thrifty I sometimes have to be
Nerve wrecking, heartbreaking, you have no care for me
Nickel and dining, from hand to hand, change sometimes is beneath

Everyone wants more of you, is there not enough to go around
Easily slips out of my hand, just stay a little longer
Enough is never enough, priorities come with demand
Envy, greed and hustling to stay afloat
Earnings outweighed by responsibilities, a few wants and many "must-pay"

You rock me, bring tears to my eyes, as I have to let go
Yielding to those in power and with control
You have not put on display what I am really worth
You loaned me a temporary smile, and left me billed with no true gain
Yearning for increase in wealth, disguised to lessen the coin shame

Scramble of Numbers

0 restraint, 1 friend, 3s a crowd, 8 drinks
Minutes you can not get back, but on constant replay
Life changing events, memorable but unwanted
At level of unacceptance, embarrassment, shame
Disappointment overwhelmingly ready to be your new face

12 it seeps in, 2 morphed into someone unknown
Dependable for others never for oneself
Blacked out, crashed, wounded and surrendered
Shackled with a lost of power and no voice
Equated to a mere criminal, degrees and work carry no weight

6 booked, pic and stamped, strip then isolated
No connection, no way out, no reasoning, no escape
Identified as a number, no face, no feeling
Ordered around, demanded with direction
Speak when granted permission, otherwise silent

10 released but never again without this label
Alone and withdrawn from help and support
Dependent on the public for assistance with life
Secret not a secret for long, beyond your control
Tough up, new deck, this hand has a new role

O.138 Blood Alcohol Level
12 am end of event
2 am accident
6 am booked
10 am released

Flashing Lights

Why did you spare my life?
To suffer in silence
Maneuver in misery
Dug further down in a ditch

Why can I not want to live?
No one knows my worth
My stretch, strength and capacity
Blinded by the burden of defeat

Who would want this for their life?
Sobbing until sick
Pills for the pain
Broken, scarred and bitter

What am I to make of what is left?
I can not see myself out of this pit
Why waste air, space with a distorted sense
My life minus life, is not theft

My heart hurts daily,
Cries in secret
Throb, is now the norm
Smile, the camera is on

Blackout

Not another. Similar day
Sleepy, everything is black, and fades away
Just a few. You know your number
Pace yourself. Soon to come deep slumber
Immobile but rolling down the dark trail
Wake up, where's your head at, reflex is snailed
Exposed. Unsafe. Crashing at a quick pace.
Stripped of rights or lost of the night with no face.
No alert. No response. Wreck but unaware.
Gather yourself. Shake it off. Fight off the stares.
Mystery black protects, shielded from the evil
Weapon disguised in wine becomes lethal
Robbed of time. Decision of regret and shamfacedness
Problems from the shaken tree I confess
Do not consume me where is the light
Refused to be burdened not giving up this fight

Storm

LIGHTENING

Comes in hot, sending vibrations throughout the atmosphere; things are never the same. Unstable, roaring furiously, many nights and days. Double-headed heart sneaks to what makes you bleed. Punishment is given, words cut deep, destruction is everywhere. Yet peace for all seems unfair.

THUNDER

Loud with no sound, talk grown and dangerous. Ready to injure, zipping across the sky, crashing all of us. Shows up when not invited, responds when not asked. Temperatures rises, low rumble expands, anywhere anytime cracks. No regrets,dismissed, quickly moved on to the next act.

CLOUDS

Height, appearance and stature with every element looks different Blue, gray, white, clear. Precious but cautious, many times back bent Everchanging bonds, important to all in many ways Unmovable, stuck. Icy. Muggy. Overtaking. Silently drifts away. Dark, towering and sharp, with all elements, The perfect storm coming and on display.

RAIN

Cry, cry, cry, isolate and retreat. No solution, no help, introvertedly dispel the heat. Powerless, weightless, intense, frequent and bound to return. The load is heavy, inside ready to explode. Drenched with tense, condense, overwhelming wet stories that are untold.

WIND

Movement in many directions determined by the climate changes. Pressured but pure, rising heat in the atmosphere has arranged this. A breezed turned hazardous, shifted frequency and intensity. Twisted, turned, fast and sometimes slow, never taking a side. Inexhaustible and gives power, reaches high, far and wide.

Shattered Dreams/Dream Snatcher

The desire is still within
And I'm still standing
The passion builds in strength
And I'm still standing

Knocked down with rejection
And I'm still standing
Betrayed with self-shame and embarrassment
And I'm still standing

Not chosen, stranger, unknown outsider
And I'm still standing
Misunderstood, misconstrued, misfit
And I'm still standing

Broken pieces, robbed of accomplishment
And I'm still standing
Disappointment to lineage
And I'm still standing

Last Time

When was the last time you made love to me
You held me
Whispered in my ear
Grabbed me close

When was the last time you kissed me
Our tongues tangoed
You stared into my eyes
Our fingers interlocked

When was the last time we played footsie
Our legs intertwined
Toes tickle with touch
Knees knock, lock and nuzzle

When was the last time you called me baby
Owned me with pride
Took control with care
Subdued with seduction

Last time, a lifetime ago
Longing in desperation
Left scarred and pained
Love-bird lullaby, love-affair

Innermy

Change your mind, change your life
Change your mind, give birth with no strife

Choose you, your peace is your ground
Choose you, once lost, seek to be found

Love yourself, it's safe and painless
Love yourself, being bold seems outrageous

Build your confidence, fearless and unmoved
Build your confidence, doubt and defeat removed

Trust in yourself, your gut speaks volumes
Trust in yourself, sweet fragrance fill rooms

Accept you, small bud starts to bloom
Accept you, errs (fault) give brief gloom

Be forgiving, mistakes lead to growth
Be forgiving, honesty and vulnerability, the new oath

No giving up, dependent are others of your kind
No giving up, your time soon come to shine

My Romeo

You were all mine
Soft and cuddly
Charming, friendly face
Spent together, all time

You protected me
Many times comforted me
Handsome as can be
At the end of the day, couldn't wait to see

Hard to see you age
What will I then be
Age alters mood
Then comes the fee

Without you, I dread
Suffering you should not see
Darkening clouds linger
Pain I wish it was given to me

You were all mine
Please do not go
My fluffy, pup
Bittersweet memories

Dinger

My side kick
Always on my heels
You walk me to the door
Separation anxiety inside you feel

Bold bark to protect
Small frame, soft to cuddle with
Fits on my hip, inside my purse
Never alone, you are my kith

Easily frightened
Startle too quick
Rip and run, chasing
Fast as a tick

New friend, many surprises
Big guard dog, tiny package
Hugs, kisses, even more kisses
Love is truly your language

Scars of Survival

Some days were about coping—
just making it through.

Never

You'll never choose me
You'll never trust me
You'll never leave, for me

You'll never be in love with me
You'll never love me like I love you
You'll never love me til death do us apart

You'll never be there, if not convenient
You'll never be unguarded, if uncomfortable
You'll never open up, if not prompted or forced

You'll never understand my tears that turn to sobs
You'll never understand ever crack leads to a shattered heart
You'll never understand to be sickly in love

You'll never match my appetite for you
You'll never value my appreciation for you
You'll never accept my respect for you

So why fight?
Why fight to be understood?
To be right and forgiven?
To be pure and precious?
To be open and honest?
To be liked and loved?

It won't change a thing.
You'll never be with me, in me and for me.
You're not mine.

Not Worth the Wait

15 minutes of your time
Absent or revoked
Not enough
Not important
I needed you

Why could you not tell
Turned your back on me again
You left with the new family
Not even a second thought
I needed you

Little girl overlooked, left behind again
Could you not see my pain
Could you not see my tears
Could you not see my heart breaking
I needed you

Your embrace was always safe
The ultimate cure for all
We loved hard, hugged every care away
Talks, were father-daughter dates
I needed you

Soaked Pillow

Crying myself to sleep, wondering if you think of me.
Crying myself to sleep, a drink is the next best thing.

I can't stop the tears from falling, they have a mind of their own.
My heart swells, floods with emotions that I'm trying to keep unknown.

Hearing your voice is soothing, as if the perfect anecdote.
Like caught mid-sea, steering, not to rock the boat.

Why aren't you here. Instead it's just this plush pillow.
As I wither, hour after hour, like a limp willow.

Can't you feel that I need you. Here with me. I plead.
Give me the time. Is it not where you want to be.

Please, just hold my heart, as it weakens in strength.
My desire to keep pushing is shortening in length.

This pillow could tell novels, like a fly on the wall.
For so many things, for so many times, it had no choice but to embrace my fall.

The silent scream, that has become a norm, still trembles from inside.
If I let it seep out, I have to look out, they would try to lock me in for a different ride.

To not see pads or a jacket, this pillow will have to do.
Please keep my secrets. My weakness. I can be honest with you.

You never sway.
Support me.
Mold to what I need.
When unable to bear, you are there.
It is guaranteed.

Moving Imprints

You are a rhythm that comes forth from deep down inside.
What I hear has a move to no end
Non-judgmental, open and expressive
You are selfless, quick and slow,
Comes in forms, intentional and direct
I can be me-hurt, broken, with a stomped mind.
Attempting to tap the away the doubt
Tempo and beat mimics my heart and pulse
Allowing me to swing, stretch, kick and vibe how I see fit
I have jumped over heartbreak
Turned away from many mistakes
Twirled into new territory as the next song sets in
You help me to flick away the pain
Converse without saying one word
Twist my defeat to be beneath me
Sway my mind to be kind to itself
I plead to let me lead and sway others to better
For my words have rippled away
Yet you never exit the stage
Point and flex until I can grasp the some hope
Bend me to break the mistrust of myself
Leap into a world that my thoughts can only imagine
Stomp my heart back to life
Rock the disgust of self away
Shake out of that slumber that holds you so tight
Lift your spirits, your soul tirelessly cries out
Speed up, increase your appetite for joy
I may tilt and fall from time to time
Roll and count until you can catch your breath and the form is right
Spot and stay focused, not looking back

It is almost curtain call, play your role in the background
Tuck away the fear, shame and guilt
Freestyling comes natural for you
Pretend the scars are silhouettes and can be unseen
Pace yourself and flow the best way you can.
Glide into being upbeat, for this is the only thing they want to see.

Sister Wife

Your heart, mind, soul is sick
Left uneasy, lost for words, side piece pick
Yell, scream, is what you want to do
Relieve this pressure, this heartache, so you can pull through

When present, the atmosphere shifts, and you are the intruder
Outsider, no ring, no kids. Soul mate type, you are not her
Untouchable, unapproachable, privileged to be in her space
Background, behind the scene, beneath her is your only place

Inadequate, incompetent, inferior in comparison, to say the least
You will never measure up, be enough, far from picture-perfect and complete
Time after time, in the slumps you lay
Floods of tears, drown my soul, inner self in disarray

Cringing, anxious, choking in shame
Wonder if I'll ever live in your similar fame
All of your "haves" are my out of reach "wants"
Heart untamed, like a puppet of a ponce

Noticed but overlooked
Present but passed over
Dedicated but devalued
Truly humble but perceived self-centered

A page from your book, may spare my name
Like a new picture worth a 1000 words, in a new frame
Fit in where you can get in, there are a few gaps I kidnap
Oiled-well machine keeps running, while I've suddenly relapsed

Until acceptance of position and scraps to be fed
Turmoil, mediocrity will be your new norm instead
You will never have, be able to hold, rule or get control
Game over, she reigns, throw in your cards and fold

65

Wife Me, Or Else

I would've...

Done anything you asked. Tried anything to have a blast.
You question my potential loyalty because the past is a huge contrast.

Were the years not enough. I tried to play tough. Sleepless nights.
Trying to prove this is not a bluff.

Settled on discarding your seed. You were pleased I did not have a rebuttal.
No title, no outings, no pressure from my end.
All of what you want, yet I feel like I'm the one in trouble.

You want your freedom.
Stray away, like a little kid in a museum.

Amazed at the sights to see
Heights and hips of every degree.

Why not just give me a chance for a sweet romance
For us to both enhance life's journey and glance
At the tests, trials, struggles and many things filed
I stood the test of times, even when things were wild.

I won't hurt you. You would only return the blow.
I'm willing to love you. We could ease into things too slow.

Just give me your heart, mind and soul.
Together we could power, just be willing to let loose control.

That's my wish as we sometimes kiss.
Hope to at some point to reminisce
Of what we are together. And could be forever.
Betrayal, dishonesty, deceit, I would never.

I will never be able to compete with family, kids and staying fit.
However, I could enhance, support, and hold things down, if you permit.

Ready to commit?

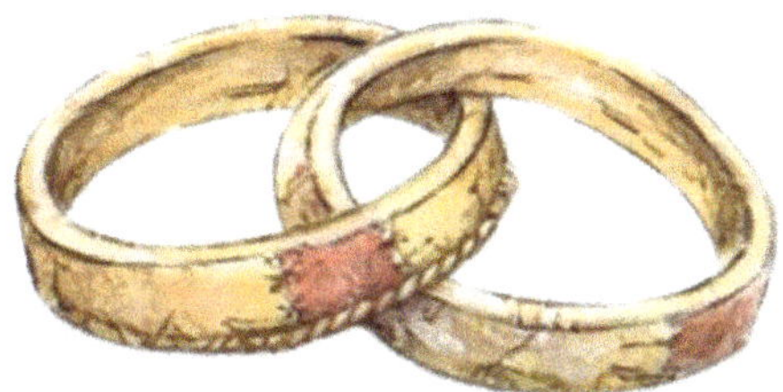

Abusive Control

You controlled her every move
You took her voice
You manipulated her
You damaged her soul
You bruised her ego
You belittled her
You never heard her out
You never took her serious
You used her as a punching bag
You got off on seeing her cry

How come home was not safe
How come I was not enough for you to stay
How was I supposed to learn love
How was I to learn to be strong
How would I learn to do different
How could you pretend like nothing happened
How could you leave our family
How could we be easily replaced
How could you not control your drinking
How could you have done better with your hands

Now I am scarred and damaged
Now I am bitter and resentful
Now I am unlovable and lonely
Now I am misunderstand and difficult
Now I am sensitive and guarded
Now I am not wanted, never chosen
Now I am angry, my words spit fire
Now I am full of doubt, no fairytale near
Now I am hurt, the one that hurts
Now I am the cycle

Church

As myself, I come
Stained, spoiled, easily influenced
Welcomed with many flaws
Encouraged to breathe through it

Glorious sounds fill the atmosphere
Electrical voices declare the king of kings
Movements usher in the presence of
He Worshippers praise and utter their offerings

Changed, unlike the times before
Straighter walk, less wicked ways
Sharing the gospel, example to be
Bring one, come all, we pray

In the same house
Serpents come to distract and destroy
Disguised in the finest of clothing
Chaos and havoc brings them joy

Divided by cliques, titles and work
All of his children, jealous in secrecy
Thirst for attention and place on stage
Festering pain and hurt spreads sneakily

Wave current of loyalty and demise of church family
Collaterally damaged, lost and confused
Retreat to my safe place, alone, where there is just one
Lay dormant once before gifts, now unused

Wanting again, a place of peace
Reverent home, to bare all and seek direction
With change comes anxiety and resistance
Now here I stand in prospection

Tug-a-Heart

You love me
You love me not.

You laid with me.
Kissed me. Touched me.
Teased me. Entered me.
Released because of me.
All selflessly. Catering.
Patient and waiting.

Not wanting to part ways but I had to throw my hands up.
You had bigger, better, more important priorities to surrender to.
Just my luck.

It doesn't dim the light on the moments we steal away with.
Not until it's a new day.
Clocks have changed.
And I'm waiting, anticipating and sit.

Where are you?
Who are you?
Why are you?
Not... reaching out, talking to me, seeing me.
Are you wanting to erase me?
Not stain the image.
That many people see.

Your words sounded good last night but your actions, today, became
something other than that.
You retreat.
You take it back.
Feels like I'm being personally attacked.

You stick to what's familiar, comfortable, what's true, what's love, what's family, what's real, what's undeniable, unforgettable, incomparable.

Your "go-to" or "partna in crime" as you would say in a bday post.
While I'm a fling, at most.
I am the afterthought, if even a thought.
Broken.
Shattered.
With a heart that is distraught.

Painful.
Yet try to breathe.
Unbearable.
Yet try to focus.
What did you expect?
You're the locust.

Intruder.
Enemy.
Wrecker.
A non-factor.
Learn your place.
Simply can be erased.

What more can I take?
Hopeless and tearful.
Lifeless and fearful.

Reality sets in,
I'll never be the chosen one.
And should be shunned.

Reasons

You would be the reason why
My birthday would be a death day

You would be the reason why
I can't breathe
I can't live
I die daily
I cry uncontrollably

You would be the reason why
You didn't love me
I didn't love me
You didn't choose me
How could I choose me

You would be the reason why
Life is not worth living
My anger boils into rage
My tears flow into sobs
My heart cracks then shatters

You would be the reason why
In your eyes, I was not the nicest
I was not the most accomplished
I was not the prettiest
I was not the total package

You would be the reason why
Love seems unattainable
Love seems far fetched
Love seems for the strong
Love is not for the sensitive

You would be the reason why
Depression was the new norm
Anxiety held on with a tight grip
Irritability fueled annoyance and impatience
Fatigue followed behind in the shadows

You were my reason why I stayed
And now,
What's the point

Addicted

I made you my drug
I craved for you year after year
I did good with you
I did even worse without you

Tolerance increased to receiving less
It was better than nothing at all
Quitting did not seem possible
Harmful to self, if she even thought to retreat

Lingering euphoric feeling like sex or taste of candy
Aids in release of daily pain, hurt, disgust
Always the right grip, hold, tone and look
Put to sleep like a baby

Lies to myself and others
Truth hidden in disguise
No control, no regrets
Acceptance of the shame and guilt

Decline in health, mental stability
Relationships rocky and withdrawn, often preferred
It was good for coping, or cutting was back up
Support was available but not first choice

About the Author

Shayla Jones is a secondary math teacher and crisis advocate who supports individuals experiencing domestic and sexual violence. Raised in a Christian home, she has navigated her own journey with depression and anxiety since adolescence while striving to meet expectations and find her place in the world.

In Scars that Speak, Shayla writes from a deeply personal space—one shaped by moments of pain, self-reflection, and the desire to release what could not be spoken aloud. What began as private writing during a dark season became a powerful outlet for healing. Her poetry reflects raw, honest conversations with herself, inviting readers to confront their own emotions with courage and compassion.

Shayla is passionate about dance, advocacy, and trauma-informed care, and she hopes her work offers others a safe and alternative path toward healing. Through her words, she seeks to remind readers that even in brokenness, growth is possible—and that choosing to face yourself is one of the bravest things you can do.